RUDOLF STEINER (1861–1925) called his spiritual philosophy 'anthroposophy', meaning 'wisdom of the human being'. As a highly developed seer, he based his work on direct knowledge and perception of spiritual dimensions. He initiated a modern and universal 'science of spirit', accessible to anyone willing to exercise clear and unprejudiced thinking.

From his spiritual investigations Steiner provided suggestions for the renewal of many activities, including education (both general and special), agriculture, medicine, economics, architecture, science, philosophy, religion and the arts. Today there are thousands of schools, clinics, farms and other organizations involved in practical work based on his principles. His many published works feature his research into the spiritual nature of the human being, the evolution of the world and humanity, and methods of personal development. Steiner wrote some 30 books and delivered over 6000 lectures across Europe. In 1924 he founded the General Anthroposophical Society, which today has branches throughout the world.

HAPPINESS

FORTUNE, SUCCESS AND THE HUMAN SPIRIT

RUDOLF STEINER

Compiled and introduced by Daniel Baumgartner

Translated by Matthew Barton

RUDOLF STEINER PRESS

Rudolf Steiner Press,
Hillside House, The Square
Forest Row, RH18 5ES

www.rudolfsteinerpress.com

Published by Rudolf Steiner Press 2017

Originally published in German under the title *Glück und Geist* by
Futurum Verlag, Basel, in 2013

A catalogue record for this book is available from the British Library

Print book ISBN: 978 1 85584 532 9
Ebook ISBN: 978 1 85584 491 9

Cover by Morgan Creative
Typeset by DP Photosetting, Neath, West Glamorgan
Printed and bound by 4Edge Ltd., Essex

Contents

Introduction

Happiness has been a human concern throughout history, inviting firstly many definitions, and then also all kinds of theories and proposals for securing it. True happiness is often coupled with its opposite. Back in the sixth century BC, Lao Tzu wrote: 'Happiness depends upon unhappiness; and unhappiness lies in wait to ambush happiness.'[1]

Good fortune and suffering, happiness and unhappiness, luck and bad luck: happiness appears to be only the 'better part' (superficially seen) of an inextricably entwined pair. If we seek happiness we must inevitably first deal with its absence. If we are blessed by good fortune we are likely to feel continually at risk from the wheel of fortune turning once again. The inconstancy of happiness cannot be relied on; and it only acquires meaning, and its due place in the flux of life, when we admit and acknowledge unhappiness as well.

In fact, we seem to have a closer connection with misfortune. Good fortune depends on either chance or effort and is only rarely unquestionably available. Our soul is by nature a Cinderella, and only comes to happiness through self-conquest—unless we are born a darling of fortune, blessed and favoured by the gods. For centuries, our ideas about fortune and misfortune have swung back and forth between endeavour and fate. How we can achieve happiness is one side of the question, but equally why some are lucky without any effort is the other. We may invite fortune to smile on us through hard work, asceticism, self-sacrifice or piety—

or it may just fall into our lap. The gods smile on us. We're 'lucky'. Happiness may be logically comprehensible, or it may also be an expression of the whims of heaven, somewhat like the weather.

What constitutes happiness is also a polarizing subject of debate: is it (re)discovering a moral core in our being, or material fortune? Happiness can mean attaining what we desire, or mastering the state of being without desires. Where happiness is concerned, idealism and materialism often come to blows. The ancient and medieval period saw happiness in terms of virtue. But since the Enlightenment, when the utilitarian 'pursuit of happiness' first became a philosophically established tenet, it was then included in the preamble to the American Declaration of Independence, and ultimately came to be seen as the hallmark of consumer culture.

In a post-religious era, our relationship with happiness alters. The Protestant-cum-capitalist God no longer rewards and blesses business acumen. And the Communist experiment to attain happiness through the spirit of the Collective has also come to naught. The cannabis road to Shangri-La in the 60s and 70s foundered in the blare of pop concerts. In the early twenty-first century, happiness is being sought instead in biology: the body is consecrated and happiness becomes the physiological property of each and every one of us. Hormones, G-spots, dopamine and the brain's pleasure systems: all of us can be little islands of happiness if we know how they function. A welcome message, no doubt, at a time of increasing insecurity and confusion.

A culture has developed that focuses on activating our resources of happiness. Not to be happy means a lack of skill in the self-management department. Self-help books have for many years now been offering a huge range of methods for attaining happiness. If we master the art of reactivating joyful moments at will, if we can map our hectic lives in flow charts, if we continually practise positive thinking, we cannot, apparently, fail to be happy. In the destabilizing conditions in which we live, we only survive by spicing life with the happiness factor. Happiness is even taught in schools. We can eat our way to happiness through an Ayurvedic diet. We can make sure our children remain happy when we divorce. Walking properly can make us happy, as can eating cutlets from happily raised pigs.

There's a pandemic of happiness breaking out. Research into happiness and positive psychology have certainly helped people cope better with difficult events—think of the progress in trauma treatment, or useful strategies to empower the disadvantaged. But though this is welcome, on the other hand the pursuit of happiness in society is creating a type of consumer who withdraws into his own endorphin sanctuary instead of really tackling social ills at their root, instead of engaging with society, nature and climate, for instance, in active and committed ways. How to increase happiness is not the key question today, at least in prosperous countries, but whether and how happiness and spirit can combine and cooperate. Rudolf Steiner's views of happiness and unhappiness can help us further here.

If you read the two lectures printed here, you will see that happiness is not Rudolf Steiner's prime concern. He is not particularly interested in how we attain happiness as such but in how we can govern the rocking vessel of our life from within. In this endeavour, happiness and unhappiness are both of equal value, helping us to work upon our outlook, to form our character and to hone our awareness of the organism of the 'I' which emerges from plural biographies.

This is a remarkable neutralization of the concept of happiness. Whether we are happy or not becomes secondary to the far more essential matter of how these both contribute to an inner stability and outlook. If we also include the idea of reincarnation, our discussion of the cause and meaning of happiness and unhappiness can unfold within a comprehensible context that illumines the sovereign importance of inner life. It becomes clear, as an overriding principle, that consciousness is not dependent on the random occurrences of life since its task is not to repulse everything negative or seek only what satisfies us, but rather to develop. This asks much of us. Only if we realize that consciousness means unceasing work upon ourselves can we properly see happiness and unhappiness as stages on a developmental path. If we think our consciousness is just a static given, we will be borne hither and thither on the changing flux of fortune and misfortune rather than embracing the evolutionary task implicit in being human.

If we seek this mission in our happiness-addicted yet frenetic age, the question still remains as to where we may find the impulse to make consciousness itself into a project of spiritual elevation and progress. We are often overtaxed, and it may seem a more urgent matter to cope with our daily lives than to use the available energy to perfect ourselves inwardly. Here lies a chasm, also apparent in the fact that Rudolf

Steiner's copious, wide-ranging ideas and suggestions have scarcely been pursued or realized. The nature of this lack is particularly apparent in relation to this theme of happiness and unhappiness: our culture either does not know or has forgotten that consciousness still has 'miles to go' in Robert Frost's phrase—a path stretching away into the far distance—and that the world really will only progress if humankind develops and enhances its consciousness. In future we will not need ever more ideas and methods of a narrowly inventive kind to solve our problems, but expansive inner experiences. It is therefore all the more important, in this respect, to hearken to Steiner's voice as he points us towards happiness of a higher kind.

In his *Autobiography*, Rudolf Steiner describes his first experience of happiness. The passage is often quoted, but it is so unusual that I would like to offer it here once more. Steiner describes his discovery of a book about geometry in his assistant schoolmaster's room:

> Soon after I joined the school at Neudoerfl, I discovered a geometry book in his room. I got on so well with this teacher that he didn't at all mind my borrowing and using it for a while. I delved into it enthusiastically. For weeks on end my soul was filled entirely by congruence, and the relationships between triangles, rectangles, polygons and so on. My thoughts kept returning to the question of where parallels actually meet; and I found the Theorem of Pythagoras spellbinding.
>
> I was profoundly satisfied to discover that one can live

inwardly in the elaboration of forms perceived purely in the soul and devoid of impressions from the outward senses. This brought me solace for the mood that had arisen in me in consequence of my unanswered questions. To be able to comprehend something purely in the mind brought me inner happiness. It is true to say that geometry brought me my first experience of happiness.[2]

It is astonishing that a nine-year-old boy could first experience happiness through geometry, especially in terms of the complete independence of inner life from outer impressions. The reverse would be more normal: to feel happiness in the enjoyment of an experience or interest belonging to the external world, something down-to-earth that manifests quite independently of any ideas brought to bear on it. In fact it was not geometry itself that gave the boy such happiness, but the mode of thinking in a mind preoccupied by geometry. As consciousness moves in a world of forms that it also simultaneously produces, working with and within it, the duality between inner and outer is reconciled. As we pursue geometric ideas we live in a unified world. While this still of course partakes of the duality of our 'real' external surroundings, to which the geometry book itself belongs, as well as, if we use them, paper, pencil and compass, these fade into insignificance beside the primary experience. Only later would Steiner come to define consciousness as one aspect of the world's totality which meets perception as the other: a process in which cognition, as he sees it, is a world-creative act arising through the union of these two.

The nine-year-old boy's experience of happiness involved confirmation of the possibility of living and functioning in the world of duality yet at the same time reconciling this duality in his inner world. Our pre-birth consciousness lives in a pre-dual state that does not entirely fade and vanish when we are born. It can be reactivated by replacing the forms of the world with the world of forms, and our participation in external reality with spiritual comprehension. Thus such happiness is founded on a sense that can be called 'spirit remembering' (a term that resurfaces in Steiner's 'Foundation Stone Meditation'): as a citizen of the earth, my inner life is not orphaned and bereft but still integrated into the spiritual world that I experienced before birth.

Later, when talking to teachers at the first Waldorf School, Rudolf Steiner was to draw attention to the deep incision in child development that becomes noticeable around the age of 8 or 9, and is connected with an experience of separation between the self and the world. The happiness Steiner experienced through geometry arose from the sense that it was possible to engender a union between I and world at precisely the age when the relationship between them is threatened. Even if the I must inevitably plunge ever further into union with the outward world and forget its spiritual roots, it can remain 'mindful of its origins'. We can think here of the Grimms fairy tale 'Hans in Luck', the happiness of whose hero turns out to be founded on the ever-diminishing worth of his earthly possessions because he always remains certain of his spiritual origins.

This first experience of happiness granted to the young Steiner involved a purity of spiritual experience. Twice he uses the word 'pure'—'purely in the soul' and 'purely in the mind'. This implies that any sensory addition to a thought is experienced as 'impure'. If we see this in alchemical and not moral terms, Steiner's preoccupation with the geometry book contributed to the first part of the process known as *solve et coagula* (dissolve and bind): the spirit is released from the wealth of random forms of the sense world to attain absolute purity, which subsequently enables it to reunite with the world at a higher level. The happiness this causes thus turns out to be the successful completion of the first part of the Great Work, which will later culminate in the spiritual renewal—which Rudolf Steiner called anthroposophy—of all cultural fields and professions.

The concept of happiness which Rudolf Steiner formed in relation to his early experiences with geometry turns out therefore to be threefold in nature. Happiness is firstly an awareness of connection with the world of spirit. Secondly it is the capacity to live in both worlds, of sense and spirit. And thirdly it is the successful fulfilment of a major part of the life task set him by destiny and himself. The young Steiner thus experiences the threefold nature of inner life as expressed in thinking, feeling and will, in its 'single package' of happiness.

Further passages on happiness in the works of Rudolf Steiner show various other aspects of the theme. His critique of the 'happiness culture' that was already emerging in his day is strikingly topical. His letters to his [first] wife Anna, who was concerned for his personal happiness, are both touching and troubling. However diverse his angles on the theme, the core of his outlook is always inner activity and fulfilling his life's task. It is important to mention this since otherwise it might seem as if Steiner had no interest in happiness but felt, rather, a secret attraction to misfortune—which certainly played its part in his life as he pursued his mission.

But it is clear that this is not so if we examine words spoken by Benedictus in Steiner's Mystery Play *The Soul's Probation*, addressed to the despairing Capesius:[3]

> If we are to understand each other,
> Accustom yourself to change the sense
> Of certain words. And do not be surprised
> If in my speech what you call pain
> Must have a different name—
> I find you fortunate.

That pain can also be called 'fortune' in another—spiritual—language; and that no doubt the reverse also applies, casts doubt on the whole terminology of happiness and unhappiness. It becomes apparent that happiness, unhappiness and spirit form a triangular structure, and only in the interplay between them does our true nature unfold. The happiness and unhappiness we encounter are united and reconciled in our heart and serve our development. What issues from our heart into the world resonates back and forth between the two poles of fortune and misfortune; and this dynamic triangle belongs to the higher mathematics of the spirit, and shows how the happiness that arose from geometry in Rudolf Steiner's experience can metamorphose into the geometry that arises from happiness. As the poet William Blake wrote:

Joy and woe are woven fine,
A clothing for the soul divine,
Under every grief and pine,
Runs a joy with silken twine.
It is right it should be so,
We were made for joy and woe,
And when this we rightly know,
Through the world we safely go.

The Essence and Appearance of Happiness

BERLIN, 7 DECEMBER 1911[4]

The teaching of repeated lives on earth is one of the spiritual-scientific insights that broad circles of our contemporaries find most difficult to relate to, along with the idea that causes we create in one life reverberate on into future lives—which we can sum up as the law of spiritual causation or karma. It is understandable that people today, with all their habits of thinking, are dismissive or dubious about such teachings. No doubt such habits of thinking will have to change before these fundamental truths of spiritual science are more generally seen as illuminating, and this will probably take a good while. But if we observe life with an open mind, considering without prejudice the things that are otherwise hard to explain in daily life, and seek the foundation that these truths can offer, we will increasingly alter our habits of thinking and come to acknowledge how insightful these great truths actually are.

Human happiness or unhappiness, or whatever names such ambiguous states are given, can certainly be counted among the phenomena we may consider here. The moment someone utters these two words, our heart resonates with an emotional response pointing us to the boundaries between our perception and what occurs outside us in the external world. This emotional response invokes an inextinguishable longing to know something about those larger, inexplicable contexts and connections that our minds, 'enlightened' in some respects, would invariably dismiss, but which a really open-minded desire for knowledge will nevertheless acknowledge. To understand what I'm saying we need only consider the sometimes enigmatic nature of happiness or unhappiness—the latter particularly—for human life. A theoretical answer is truly not adequate to resolve the enigma. More is needed to resolve it than a mere theory, than anything produced by what we can call an external, abstract science. There is no doubt at all, is there, that we feel in our soul a strong impulse to live in some kind of accord and harmony with our surroundings. But there is nothing more clearly in discord than someone who can say, or whose fellows say of him, that he is plagued by misfortune throughout his life. This acknowledgement is quickly followed by asking why this might be so—a question that is of deep, incisive importance for the whole value of human life and for the powers too that underlie our life.

Robert Hamerling, an important nineteenth-century poet who, sadly, received far too little recognition, wrote a little essay 'On Happiness'. He begins this with a memory which, as he says, repeatedly rises in him whenever he considers the question of happiness. He heard this anecdote in Venice. Whether it is fictitious or not is of no importance to him. It goes like this:

A couple had a little girl, but the wife died a few days after childbirth. On the day the child was born, the father heard that he had lost his whole fortune in a shipwreck, and he died of the shock on the very day of his daughter's birth. Thus the child was an orphan from the very outset. A rich relative first fostered her, and in her will bequeathed her a large fortune, but she died while the child was still very young, and when they opened the will they found it contained an error. The will was disputed and the child lost everything she had been due to inherit. She grew up in poverty and need, and had to take work as a maidservant. Now a very kind, warm-hearted lad fell in love with her, and she too liked him very much. Their connection lasted some while, and it must have seemed to the girl, whose life had brought her such difficulties, that some happiness could at last be hers. But it turned out that her beloved was of the Jewish faith and that the marriage therefore could not go ahead. She bitterly accused him of deceiving her, but she could not let him go. A curious flux and inter-play is always apparent in her life. The lad could not give up the girl either, and he promised to get himself bap-tized as soon as his father died, which would surely not be too long, and then they could get married. His father did fall ill soon after and the son was called to his sickbed in a far-off place. Now, among all the other pains the girl had to endure, she too fell gravely ill. The father of her bridegroom had died in the meantime. Her fiancé got himself baptized, but when he came back to her the girl had already died from a combination of her physical ailments and inner sufferings. He found his bride dead, and was seized with the bitterest pain. Although the girl had already been buried, he had an irresistible urge to see her once more, and he did finally succeed in getting her body exhumed. But when the coffin was opened they found her in a position that showed clearly she had been buried alive: she had woken up in her grave and turned upon her side!

Robert Hamerling said that he kept recalling this tale whenever people talked about human misfortune, or when he thought about it, and about how it sometimes seemed that a person could be plagued by misfortune from the cradle to the grave, and even beyond it, as in this case. The story might be a legend of course, but that matters little since we can all recognize that such a thing might have happened, even if this particular story is not true. It offers a vivid illustration of the great and fearful question as to *why* someone might continually meet with such misfortune. And in fact this can make us aware that it may be impossible to speak of happiness or unhappiness at all if we consider only a single human life. At the very least, we might acknowledge that our habits of thinking might need to change to encompass more than a single life when we reflect on the great disparity between our sense of the value of human life and what such a person, plagued by misfortune, is compelled to endure in the world, and in her close interplay with it, between birth and death. It really seems here that we must raise our gaze to look beyond the boundaries of birth and death.

But when we take a closer look at the word happiness, or unhappiness, we immediately see that it can be used only in a certain sphere. While there is much in the world around us that reminds us of our inherent accord or discord with the world, we can scarcely speak about happiness or unhappiness in relation to other analogous occurrences. Think of a crystal, which develops regular forms in accordance with specific laws but can be compelled, through its proximity to other crystals, or by other forces of nature acting in its vicinity, to form one-sidedly. It can fail to form the angles and edges that it would by nature form if it were unimpeded. And therefore there are very few perfectly formed crystals in nature that give full expression to the laws at work in them. Or think of a plant, in which a formative law is also inherent. But almost invariably, plants fail to fully unfold their inner developmental impulse in the face of wind, weather and other environmental factors. The same is true of animals. We can go still further, in fact, and recognize how many germinal life forms die before they develop, never fully unfolding because external conditions do not allow them to become what their inner disposition seeks to be. Let us recall the huge number of ocean creatures that never get beyond their germinal stages—how few of them actually develop into the creatures that populate the oceans. We can put it like this: it is clear that the life forms and creatures we find in the various kingdoms of nature have inner formative forces and laws at work in them, but that the latter encounter hindrances, obstacles in their surroundings and therefore often cannot live in full harmony and accord with their environment. When we come to speak of human happiness or unhappiness, we cannot overlook this fact and its relevance to our own condition. Here we find that people cannot fulfil and realize their inherent capacities because of all the hindrances that stand in their way. Or sometimes perhaps, like a crystal—and I mean this only metaphorically—a person may be fortunate enough to develop his free and full range of angles and corners, and can say that nothing hinders him; that outer conditions and circumstances help him to develop what lies within him as the inner core of his being. Only in this case do people usually feel lucky and happy. Anything else will either leave them indifferent or compel them to say they are unhappy or unfortunate. But unless we succumb to fantasy, we cannot say that crystals, plants or even all the countless germinal life forms in the ocean that never develop suffer misfortune or unhappiness in consequence. And in human life, too, we can soon find that there is a limit beyond which we can no longer speak of happiness or unhappiness even if external factors affecting us initially appear to have a destructive or obstructive effect. Do we even speak of misfortune or unhappiness in relation, say, to a great martyr who seeks to assert some important cause in the world and dies by the hand of his enemies? In fact we don't. Giordano Bruno is one such example; he was burned at the stake. We can feel here that there is something within a person himself that is no longer a matter of mere misfortune or—when a cause is successful—fortune. We see, therefore, that happiness or unhappiness are confined to the human domain, but within this they apply only within narrower confines.

Let us now approach this realm of our feeling of happiness or unhappiness. It soon becomes apparent that this concept is hard to grasp hold of. You may remember the story of Diogenes—which may likewise be based on a legend. Alexander invites him to ask for a request, a favour. And Diogenes, as few others would have dared to do, asks Alexander to move aside since he is blocking his sun. At that moment, sunshine was what he wished for, what would make him happy. Others would have thought of other things they lacked. But let us continue. The happiness of someone who always seeks enjoyment, who thinks his life is only happy if all the desires rising from his passions and drives are satisfied—this happiness of his cannot surely be in any way the same as that of the ascetic who hopes to perfect his nature, who thinks life is only valuable if he denies himself all kinds of things, even perhaps subjecting himself to pain and suffering that ordinary fortune and misfortune might very likely spare him. How different, therefore, are ideas of happiness and unhappiness in an ascetic or someone who indulges every desire. Every concept of happiness we formulate easily proves inadequate. We need only think here of how unhappy someone can be when jealous without reason, without a real basis of fact for this jealousy. Let us imagine someone with unjustified jealousy who believes he has all kinds of reasons for this feeling. He will be profoundly unhappy, and without any outward reason for being so. Yet the degree and intensity of his unhappiness has nothing to do with outward reality but only with the way in which the person concerned relates to reality, in this instance based on compete illusion.

At the beginning of the first volume of Jean Paul's unfinished memoirs *Flegeljahre,* the writer shows us that both happiness and unhappiness can be highly subjective, and invariably point us away from external reality into our inner life. He relates how someone who usually lives in central Germany imagines what it would be like for him to become a priest in Sweden. He paints himself a wonderful picture of this possibility—of sitting in his parsonage and witnessing the day growing dark at 2 in the afternoon; of the people coming to church in the dark, each with their own candle. This reminds him of his childhood when his siblings likewise all had their own candle. This picture he conjures of people coming to church through the darkness is a dreamy fantasy. Likewise he daydreams of other situations summoned simply by certain natural conditions—for example he pictures himself in Italy, imagining that he sees orange trees. All this transports him into a mood of the most wonderful happiness, yet it bears no relation whatever to reality. It is all just a dream.

I am sure that with this dream of being a priest in Sweden Jean Paul is pointing to deep questions relating to happiness and unhappiness. Basically he is showing that these questions can be redirected from the outer world to our inner life. Curiously, since happiness and unhappiness can be entirely dependent on our own perception, we here see a universal concept of happiness vanish from view. And then again, when we examine what people usually think of as their happiness or unhappiness, in innumerable cases they relate these feelings not to their inner world but to outer circumstances. Indeed, we might even say that the distinctive thing about the human need for happiness is that it is deeply rooted in our continual urge not to feel alone and isolated with our thinking, feeling and whole inner growth, but in harmony with what lives and works in our surroundings. People basically speak of good fortune, when they want to discount it as due solely to themselves—instead ascribing it to something outside them. Here we could consider the luck of a gambler or card player, for no doubt the biggest and most trivial things are connected. However paradoxical it seems, we can connect a player's luck, and pleasure at this, with the satisfaction felt by someone who makes a discovery or gains an insight. You see, when we gain knowledge of something this summons in us a sense that our thinking, our inner life, is in harmony with the world, that what is outside us is also comprehended within us; and therefore that we are not isolated and alone, staring blankly at the world as a great enigma, but that our inner life has responded to what is outside us. The pleasure we feel in knowledge and insight derives, really, from a living inner connection with the outer world, a sense that what is outside us is rekindled within and reflected there, that the outer may have something to do with the inner, proven by their accord. If we analyse the pleasure of the gambler or card player, likewise, even if he himself is unaware of this, we find it would not exist if he himself could make what happens happen. His pleasure arises from the fact that something outside him happens without his effort, that the world in a sense takes notice of him, that it brings him something that benefits him, that in this one instance at least it shows that he is not separate from it but has a certain connection and contact with it. And when he loses, his unhappiness at his 'run of bad luck' is based really on the lack of this sense. Unhappiness triggers in him a feeling of being excluded from the world, as if it took no notice of him and had broken off the contact.

In brief, then, it is not right at all to think that happiness or unhappiness is only something confined within us, but rather that these feelings can create a connection in the profoundest sense between ourselves and the world. This is why people in our enlightened times so easily become more superstitious about good luck than about anything else—absurdly super-stitious and expectant that some powers or whatever they might be called, elements that lie outside them, will come to their aid. This hope and expectancy can make people very superstitious. I once knew a very rational and enlightened German poet who was writing a play. He knew in advance that the play would not be ready by the end of a certain month. Yet he believed that the play would only succeed if he submitted it to the relevant theatre director before the first of the following month. His superstition was that if he did not meet this deadline, the play would be a failure. As the month was drawing to a close I was walking along the street by chance one day, knowing from conversations with the writer that he was nowhere near finishing his play, when I saw him cycling to the post office like a man possessed. I waited, and when he emerged from the post office he said to me: 'I've sent it off.' I asked, 'Is it finished then?' He said, 'I still have to work on the final act, but I've sent it off already because it will, I believe, only be a success if I get it to the director by the end of the month. But I added a note to say that they should send it back to me when they get it, and I will finish writing it. But I had to send it off now!' Here we see someone who does not rely on what he himself can achieve, thinking that his powers alone, his hard work or energy, do not suffice but that the world outside him must help. He believes that the world knows something of him and therefore he does not stand there alone, isolated as a single, separate soul.

All this only demonstrates that the concept of happiness in general easily evades our grasp. It evades our grasp likewise when we look for what authors have written about it, for they are of course concerned in some way or other with their written formulations. We all recognize, don't we, that we can only speak about things we have a real, living relationship with, not just a theoretical one. Philosophers or psychologists who write about happiness really only have a living relationship with the happiness or unhappiness they themselves have experienced. Now a factor we must certainly place in the scales here is that knowledge itself, as we find it working in the external human world, already signifies a kind of happiness in a higher sense. Anyone who has ever felt the inner delight that understanding or knowledge can give will acknowledge this. The most outstanding philosophers, from Aristotle onwards into our own times, have testified to the special happiness that derives from wisdom or knowledge. But at the same time we have to ask ourselves whether such an answer has any meaning for someone who labours down a dark mine, say, for weeks on end with little respite, whose life is spent in the most dire conditions. Is there any link between this philosophical interpretation of happiness and what lives in the soul of someone compelled to spend his life in physical drudgery? Life offers us a remarkable answer to the question of happiness. We can find endless examples to show that philosophical answers to this question can become curiously distanced, I would say grotesquely so, from what we can encounter in ordinary daily life when we try to perceive its real and actual nature. And then life teaches us other things about happiness too, and from these different perspectives can itself appear curiously contradictory in relationship to happiness. Let me give one instance that can stand for many others.

Let us imagine someone who cultivates what we can call higher ideas, someone with a distinctive capacity of imagination, who has to undertake work of a tedious, unedifying kind. Let us say that he spends almost his whole life as a common soldier. I haven't made this up, I'm thinking of an actual instance—the case of a very remarkable person: Josef Emanuel Hilscher, born in Austria in 1806, who died in 1837. He spent most of his life serving as a common soldier, and despite his great gifts gained no advancement in the ranks. At his death, this man left a great number of poems, not only skilful in form but imbued with deep qualities of soul, and also excellent translations of the work of the English poet Byron. The man had rich sensibility, and we can try to imagine the gulf that existed between whatever happiness daily life brought him and what he experienced inwardly. His poems are not burdened by pessimism but full of strength and richness. They show us that despite the inevitable disappointments of such a life it nevertheless broadened out into a kind of eternity and was raised inwardly to joyfulness. It is a shame that humankind so easily overlooks or forgets such an instance, for if we give it some thought we can discover, perhaps—since things only differ in degrees—that it is possible for a person to create an inner foundation of happiness even where his outward life seems wholly devoid of it.

Now especially from the perspective of spiritual science, if one gets no further with it than misconceptions or primitive outlooks, people might rage fanatically against the very idea of happiness or try to explain all life narrowly through the idea of repeated lives on earth and karma. It would be fanatical and misconceived to think that all striving for happiness and good fortune is merely egoism, and that spiritual science ought to lead us beyond such thoughts. Even Aristotle thought it ridiculous to claim that the virtuous man should somehow learn to be happy in the midst of inexplicable suffering. This is because we shouldn't see happiness only as an egoistic pleasure. Even if this may be so initially, this does not render it worthless for humanity's whole advancement. We can also regard happiness as bringing our soul faculties into harmony and therefore encouraging their general development, whereas unhappiness creates disharmony in us and can prevent us from fully unfolding our abilities and strengths. Even if we initially seek happiness to satisfy our egoism, it can still be seen as cultivating a harmonious inner power in us. Someone who acquires this inner harmony of soul through happiness may, one can hope, gradually conquer his egoism, whereas someone plagued only by unhappiness will less easily get beyond his self-concern. And on the other hand, when someone seeks happiness and gains it as an egoistic fulfilment, the fact that his powers and faculties gain harmony means that he can also be a force for good to others. We therefore shouldn't disparage what we can call happiness. That is a narrow view. But it is likewise mistaken, a shallow view of spiritual science, to think that someone who is unhappy, or happy, has inevitably caused this himself through karma from a previous life. We're on tricky ground here because this can also be true. But karma—that is, the law of causation passing from one life to the next—cannot be seen only in simple, explanatory terms. We have to regard it, rather, as something that penetrates our will and leads us to live in accordance with this law. We are only justified in thinking in these terms if this law enhances and enriches life itself. We have seen that people initially conjure in themselves a compelling desire for happiness in an effort to overcome their isolation, and to have within them something of the world's outer realities, a sense that they partake of these realities and are encompassed by them. On the other hand, we have also seen that happiness can be something that exists in crass contrast to outward realities, and survives only through a person's own perception and experience of these realities.

How can we reconcile this apparent contradiction in a way fully informed by reality itself and not only through abstractions and theories? We can do so if we turn our mind, and our spiritual gaze, to what we can call the inner core of our being. In previous lectures we have seen that this core being of ours works upon our outer form and nature, that it shapes our body itself yet also places us into the world at a particular location and in particular circumstances. Let us keep this inner core of ours in mind and ask this question: what can its relationship be to our happiness or unhappiness? We can most easily answer this if we remember that the fortunes and misfortunes we encounter are intended by ourselves. I myself wanted this or that to happen. I also steered my wisdom, my sagacity in a direction where this or that could occur, but now I see by what has in fact happened that the success of this intention far exceeds what I could have foreseen or predetermined. Particularly those who hold responsible positions in the world will offer countless instances of efforts and endeavours far outmatched by the ensuing success of a venture. If we do not think of the core of our being simply as a given but, in terms of spiritual science, as being involved in ongoing development—if we think of it as shaping not only our present life but many succeeding lives, and creating our life as it now is, we will see that when this inner core crosses the threshold of death it will traverse a supersensible world and, when the time comes, will engage again in a new physical existence. If we see our core being in these terms, within a world-view of this kind, what will be our stance towards some success or good fortune that has come our way? We will never say that we have been fortunate and are now satisfied, that the powers we ourselves set in motion aimed to achieve far less than we actually achieved, and that this was simply a matter of good fortune. Someone who seriously credits karma and repeated lives on earth, and who seeks to make his life accord with the workings of karma, will never say such a thing. Instead he will say: success has come, but my own powers were weak in comparison with it. Rather than being satisfied with my success, I will learn to enhance my capacities further in consequence. I will plant seeds within the core of my being that can lead it further towards ever greater perfection. My undeserved success, my good fortune, shows me what I lack, my inadequacies. I must learn from it. Someone who properly considers karma and credits it can respond to success and good fortune in no other way. Good fortune comes his way, not by chance, not randomly, but as a kind of gift which he does not regard as an end in itself but as a beginning, a first step he can learn from, which casts its light before him on the path he pursues into future states of his developing being.

But what is the opposite of what we have just said? Let's

picture this clearly. Someone who believes in repeated lives, in reincarnation and karma, or in spiritual causation, will feel that success and good fortune are seeds of capacity, that they spur him on to see success as a beginning only, a cause at work in his future development. The opposite of this would be regarding some misfortune that comes our way as not merely accidental. If we see human life as extending beyond a single lifetime, we can regard misfortune as an end or culmination, as something whose causes must be sought in the past just as the effects of good fortune can be pursued into our future development. So we regard unhappiness and misfortune as the effect of our own development. Why is this?

A comparison can shed light on this, and shows that we ourselves cannot always properly judge the causes at work in our lives. Let us imagine someone who, until the age of 18, has lived lazily from his father's wealth, but in his own estimation has been very happy. When he is 18 his father loses his fortune, and the son is now compelled to learn a proper trade and no longer to sponge off his father. To begin with this is painful and hard for him—'Oh, such misfortune,' says the son. But is he really seeing his own fate here in the right light? If he now learns a proper profession, by the age of 50 he may look back and see that what he regarded as a grave misfortune at the time was so only for his father, not for him. If this had not happened he might have remained a ne'er-do-well all his life. Because of this stroke of 'misfortune', in fact, he became a decent person, the person he now is.

So let us ask this: when does this person properly judge his fate? At 18, when misfortune strikes, or at 50, when he looks back at what appeared unfortunate? If he ponders this further and asks what was the real cause of his misfortune when he was 18, he can discover that he might easily have been spared it. Outwardly it seems as if the misfortune was caused only by his father losing all his wealth. But if, let us say, he had been very eager to work and learn from childhood on, achieving a great deal without any outer compulsion so that the loss of his father's fortune was not problematic for him, things would have looked very different at that time, and he himself would have suffered no misfortune. He might therefore say: 'The cause of my bad luck seems to lie outside me, but in fact its deeper cause lies within. The way I lived meant that life faced me with misfortune, pain and suffering. I myself caused it.'

When someone says this to himself, he has already to some small degree understood that everything we outwardly encounter is caused by inner factors. We can regard what happens to us as being caused by our own development. All misfortune is something which we can see came to us because we ourselves are imperfect. Misfortune tells us that something in us is not yet as perfect as it should be. Here we have the opposite circumstances from those at work in success. We see misfortune as the end of what a former stage of our development brought about, what we ourselves brought about then. And when we do not lament misfortune as something for which the external world is to blame, but instead ponder on the inner core of our being and seriously credit its causes in past lives, and thus in karma, then we regard it as a prompting to us to increasingly perfect ourselves, to learn from life—to see life as a school. But when we see things like this, karma and what we call the law of reincarnation, can give us strength in life and make it richer and fuller.

Now the question arises as to whether mere knowledge of the law of karma can enhance and enrich life, and if this is the case whether, in a sense, it can create good fortune from misfortune. However strange this may sound to many people nowadays, I would like to say something that can be significant for the whole spiritual-scientific view of happiness and unhappiness. Let's recall the legend related by Hamerling, about the girl who was plagued by misfortune until her dying day and, since she ended up being buried alive, even beyond the grave. Without entering more deeply into the powers knowledge can give us, what I am about to say may well seem paradoxical. But let us assume, hypothetically for a moment, that this girl had found herself in surroundings where a spiritual-scientific outlook prevailed, so that those around her were aware that a core spiritual being lives within each of them: an essence that exists before birth and lives on after death and reveals, through what each person is and can accomplish in the outer world, the effects of previous lives, as well as enabling us to acquire new powers and capacities for future lives. Let us imagine that the girl had such insight, as a power within her soul—this is perfectly conceivable. Such ideas enhance faith in the inner strength of the core of our being, and this inner strength can then emanate from the soul and spirit and work into our corporeal nature [...] and in this case it could have strengthened the girl's health so that, through the power of such faith, she might have survived until her fiancé returned after the death of his father. This may seem paradoxical to anyone who does not know what power is possessed by a knowledge and insight rooted in reality, which are therefore not merely abstract and theoretical but also live and work in the soul as a germinal power.

As regards questions of happiness this may offer little comfort to those who really have to spend the whole of their lives in work that never fulfils them, and must suffer lifelong from a quashing of their hopes. Yet we can see that such a strong faith in the essential core of our being, a faith which knows that this single human life is just one among many, can nevertheless awaken strength within us. In the inner sanctum of the soul, as I grasp my spiritual nature, my connection with the whole world into which I have been placed can explain to me what I encounter in the outer world as initially inexplicable happiness or unhappiness, as easy or a difficult destiny. Ordinary words of comfort cannot help us cope with misfortune when it strikes us. What can help us, though, is a capacity to see what we suffer as a link in the chain of existence. Then we say that considering only one link means seeing only appearance and not reality, just as the young man of 18 saw only appearance when he suffered what he thought was misfortune, which turned out to be the cause of his subsequent happiness. When we look more deeply, we find that when viewed from a certain, narrower angle instances of happiness or unhappiness offer us only appearance, but when we enlarge our perspective and place these experiences in the overall context of human life they reveal their true meaning and nature. But if we were to see this overall context of human life as confined within the bounds of birth and death, we could never explain why someone should suffer destitution or be compelled to forego the fulfilment in life and work enjoyed by others. The reality of such things can only be explained through spiritual science, for, in a phrase often spoken but only gaining its true meaning for human destiny through the light of spiritual science, 'What we comprehend has no power over us any longer.' Someone who, in the core of his being, sees success and happiness only as a spur to higher development will also regard misfortune in similar terms. The seeming contradiction is resolved when we move on from a view of happiness and unhappiness as something that happens *to* us, and instead focus on how we can inwardly transform our experiences and what we can make of them.

If we have learned from the law of karma not only to feel pleasure in success but to regard it as a prompting to us to develop further, we can also see lack of success and misfortune in the same way. Everything is transformed in the human soul, and the appearance of happiness or unhappiness turns to reality within us. This is extraordinarily significant. Imagine this: a person strongly objects to the idea of reincarnation and observes how someone suffers from unfounded jealousy, say, due to pictures his fantasy creates, or how someone else gives himself up to a dream of happiness; or, on the other hand, how someone else makes an inner reality for himself out of mere appearance, not one grounded in actual circumstances, yet a state that does become inwardly very real to him. Such a person could at least acknowledge how incredibly wrong and inappropriate it would be in relation to the outer world for these inner realities to occupy the whole of a person's only life, without further resolution. When someone crosses the threshold of death, his concepts of reality are also doubtless extinguished, his jealousy or illusions of happiness. But the pleasure and suffering that have informed his soul, that have manifested in the motions of his sensibility, become a power within him, live a life in the soul that is connected with his further development in the world. Through the transformation I have described, therefore, we see how the human being is indeed called upon to turn appearance into reality.

Here we arrive at an explanation of what was said at the outset, that we cannot immediately ascribe good fortune that comes to us from without to our I, our core individuality. The fortunate circumstances that come our way and enhance our life can however be inwardly transformed by us so that what is initially outward appearance becomes inner reality. By virtue of this transformation we can turn external appearance into actuality, reality. But looking around us we see that crystals, plants and animals cannot fully unfold the laws at work in them either, that they meet outward hindrances. We spoke of the countless seeds or germinal life forms that go under to let some survive and develop. Why can we not speak here of fortune or misfortune in the same way as we do in relation to human life? It is because here something outward does not become inward so that external reality is reflected within, so that appearance can be transformed into real being. It is only because we possess an essential core being within us that we can detach ourselves from immediate, outward reality and experience a new reality. This new, inwardly experienced reality differs from that of mundane life in so far as we can say this: on the one hand my life comes to me through heredity, a line of descent that endows me with characteristics inherited from parents, grandparents and so on. But I live too in a spiritual legacy of causation that can give me something other than the happiness or good fortune I meet in the external world. Here it becomes apparent that we belong to two worlds at once, an outer and inner world. You can call this dualism if you like, but the very way in which we can turn appearance into being, into reality, shows that this dualism likewise is only an apparent one. Within us, outward appearance is continually transformed into inner reality. And life further shows us that what we experience in our imagination when we 'wrongly' interpret the facts becomes a reality within us.

Thus we find that what we call happiness and unhappiness are closely tied up with our inner being—closely bound up too with the inner being which, in the spiritual-scientific world-view, is seen to pass through a series of lives on earth. Seen in this light, we can say, surely, that all outward appearance of happiness is only the *foundation* for an inner happiness that becomes an imperishable possession as we evolve. All outward happiness that comes our way is wonderfully characterized in the legend of Croesus. Solon says to Croesus that no one should vaunt his own happiness until his life ends, for all outward happiness can alter. Good fortune can turn to misfortune. What is the happiness that can never be taken from us? Whatever we ourselves make of our outward fortunes, whether successes or disappointments. And so our whole relationship to good fortune is truly encapsulated in that lovely, true proverb, that 'We make our own fortune', or that 'Fortune helps them that help themselves'. There are many beautiful and really very apt proverbs about luck and fortune, and they show us the deep wisdom of ordinary folk. Those who think themselves the most educated could learn an infinite amount from such wisdom. Sometimes these truths are couched in fairly earthy terms. There's a proverb that 'Even the gods battle in vain with a man's stupidity'. But in another proverb this same stupidity is connected with good fortune: 'A stupid fellow has the greatest luck.' This does not mean that the gods seek to tempt us away from our failings by showering us with good fortune. No, in fact this proverb reveals a clear sense of the need to internalize our relationship with outward good fortune in the world, for our wisdom, if it relates only to outward things and outward circumstances, will not help us much. What helps is the wisdom that has become transformed and internalized and thus acquires a quality possessed by the naive and native intuition of a simple person, founded on the strong core of his inward being that goes beyond birth and death and is only explicable in the light of repeated lives on earth. Everything we can experience as happiness in the external world basically can be divided into mere semblance of happiness and true happiness, its real essence. The latter arises only when we can make something of life's outward circumstances by transforming them and incorporating them into the evolving core of our being, which passes from one life to the next. And when someone—Herder it was—is in the deep throes of sickness and pain, we can understand what he means when he says to his son, 'Give me a great, beautiful idea, and that will reinvigorate me!' This gives a tangible sense of Herder's perception that a great and beautiful thought can shine in to our torment and vitalize us, his expectation, really, of happiness from such a source. It is easy to say, perhaps too glibly, that a person must create his own luck within him; but if we consider, in regard to matters we have touched on today, that a spiritual-scientific outlook has power and efficacy beyond merely theoretical knowledge, encompassing the soul-spiritual core of our being, and filling it with all that underlies the semblance of happiness and unhappiness, then this world-view, like scarcely any other, can inform our thoughts with grandeur. Such thoughts can enable us, when misfortune has made our life almost unendurable, to fill ourselves with the thought that this is only one part of the totality of life!

We looked at this question of happiness today to show how real thoughts about life's whole context, as spiritual science conveys them, can fire and fertilize ordinary daily life. Such thoughts are not pale and theoretical but can really affect our life, can introduce a living power into it. That is the important thing. Rather than looking for merely outward comfort when misfortune strikes us from without, we should learn to bear it by awakening inner powers. We must seek to put others in touch with the real inner powers that lead us beyond the realm of misfortune to another that belongs to it, even if life seems to contradict this. But this insight comes only from a body of knowledge, a science, that shows that human life extends beyond birth and death, and is in fact intimately connected with everything that creates the enlivening ground of our universe. Such a world-view can fill our subtle apprehensions with a sense that the life in which we stand is like a ship battered by storms and seething waves, yet we find within us the courage to found upon our own inner being the stability that nothing in the outer world gives us in the same way. Today's reflections can perhaps set before us an ideal

that Goethe to some degree prefigured, though we can lead it
further, beyond the intimation that filled Goethe, towards a
human ideal that holds true for all: not something that is
immediately or directly realized in a single lifetime, but an
ideal for all human life when we feel ourselves rocked and
battered like a ship in a stormy sea, but can retain trust in our
inner being. With a slight modification to Goethe's words,
this can conveyed as follows:

> At the wheel a man stands bold
> While wind and waves are battering the ship—
> Wind and waves and not his soul.
> He masters them—looks down into the deep
> Turmoil of the sea; and whether or not he sink
> Or reach the shore, he harbours trust
> In powers alive within his inmost breast.

Spirit Knowledge in Glad and Grave Moments of Life

BERLIN, 15 JANUARY 1915[5]

It is perfectly understandable that people in our time, naturally inclined to materialistic thinking, will find it absurd and
paradoxical when spiritual enquiry states that the human
being is more than external science acknowledges, that we
are more than biology, physiology and psychology admit, the
latter founded likewise on external facts. Spiritual enquiries
lead to the assertion that we are in fact composed of a
complex of aspects of which the physical, material body is
only one, while the others—only perceptible to spiritual
enquiry as I said—live in an invisible, supersensible realm,
and from there work and act upon us. It is perfectly natural
that people today ridicule such an idea, that they rail against
the idea that we have besides the physical body, which serves
us in the sense world when we act outwardly and perceive
things in that world, also subtler bodies, subtler aspects of
human nature. Spiritual science tells us that we have, apart
from our physical body, an 'etheric body', which is 'subtler'
in comparison to the grosser physical body; and that these
two aspects of human nature are the ones that remain in the
physical realm when we immerse ourselves in the unconscious state of sleep. It further tells us of higher aspects, more
spiritual constituents, which we call the astral body and the I,
and states that these pass over into a world of spirit when we

fall asleep. Spiritual science shows that these higher aspects of human nature, resting in an unconscious realm during sleep, are in fact the real, active agencies that ensoul and give strength to the physical and etheric bodies when we awaken from sleep again.

The inability of modern science to acknowledge these higher aspects of human nature resembles a person's failure to accept that air exists because he cannot see it or touch it. We inhale and exhale material air in quick succession, and in the same way—if we understand the word 'breathe' in a metaphorical sense—our physical and etheric bodies breathe in the astral body and I when we wake up, and breathe them out when we fall asleep. As we fall asleep our physical body releases the astral body and I into the world of spirit. This spiritual knowledge becomes fruitful when we apply it in life, when our soul can be imbued by it and can regard life in this light.

As human beings we are sustained by the current of life, which bears us onwards between birth and death. This onward stream of life is something I would like to clarify with a comparison. When we sit in a train compartment and look out of the window, it first seems to us—if we're not used to train travel—that the trees and houses outside are rushing past us. This is roughly how we live on our journey through life, with our views of the world and our feelings, in relation to happiness and unhappiness, to luck and misfortune, success and lack of it. How do happiness and unhappiness, good fortune and misfortune work upon our human nature? Just as human nature is initially formed by what it can draw from the external physical world, so happiness and unhappiness, success and bad luck in a sense always draw on our feelings about the world, our feelings about life so that, in these feelings and emotions of ours, we seem to witness the world itself passing before us: our pain or suffering seems to rush towards us. We gradually have to learn that this passage of the world is only an apparent one, that it is only seemingly passing before us. It is up to us to find the right standpoint here, to learn to see, as we are borne onwards through life, that in fact we can remain tranquil in our feelings about the world and about life: that we can rest in the world of spirit when happiness and suffering, success or lack of it, seem— and only seem—to set the world in motion and our feelings with it.

We must also consider that humanity is continually evolving through succeeding epochs, giving rise to ever new and developing experiences; that our soul experiences different things in different eras of humanity's evolution. According to these changing experiences, therefore, our feelings about life, our whole sense of things also changes. To find inner peace and contentment within the rushing current of life, a person today needs a different relationship to the world from the one the human soul could have in former times. Spiritual science shows us that a certain sum of powers, a kind of treasury, a source of spiritual life, resides today in human souls. These powers seek to emerge, rather than to stay concealed in the soul: they seek to appear in human consciousness so that we feel them to be not just an inner urge, an inner imperative, but something we can incorporate into our thinking, our world of ideas. How exactly does spiritual science speak to humankind today? It does not seek to bear messages from alien realms of existence, from strange foreign lands as it were, but it speaks in a way that tries only to tell each soul what already resides deep within it. The spiritual researcher is, basically, convinced that there is something present in each and every soul that he tries only to clothe in outward concepts and ideas, and that therefore he says nothing to people other than what they already bear within them. The whole of spiritual science, when the spiritual enquirer presents it to humankind in the right way, seeks to offer only what already rests in the deep stratum of each and every human soul. And therefore this science of the spirit is only a prompting to every soul to draw forth what resides within it.

A whole sum of powers rests in these depths of the human soul; and only when these are drawn up into our awareness do they show what acts within us, what inwardly pervades and lives in our soul. The human being is truly richer, fuller, than he often thinks.

There is a remarkable law governing our relationship with knowledge and perception of the world and, when we know it, it can give us deep insights into many enigmas of the human soul. To clarify this in the simplest way, I'd like to refer again to a reality that spiritual science can investigate; and this is that every time we fall asleep we send our higher being—the I and astral body—into a world of spirit. To begin with we are unable to perceive anything in this world of spirit, but the aspects of ourselves we send out into it really do to a large extent contain, and are composed of, what spiritual science seeks to draw forth from deep sources of existence and reveal to the waking mind. Only in ordinary, daily life is it true to say that when we sleep, when, in the state of sleep, we are outside our physical and etheric body, do we succumb to unconsciousness that conceals what resides in our soul. And when we wake up again, and bring our I and astral body back into the physical and etheric body, this I and astral body are again filled with the impressions received by outer sense perception of the material world. In waking life our soul is given up to the external world. And just as, at night, unconsciousness dims awareness of what rests in the depths of the soul, so during the day these impressions of the external, material world are what do so. Yet in the depths of the soul there really does rest and reside everything that spiritual science seeks to make people aware of. Now this law I mentioned is a very important, significant one, and gradually one can come to see that it governs all existence. The law is this: that what can be greatly beneficial in one condition can have a ruinous effect in another, different condition or, if you like, at a different locus.

Invisible, supersensible forces reside in what remains hidden to people in their material awareness. These forces reside in what we discharge into the world of spirit in sleep; they rumble within this inner being of ours and introduce uncertainty, lack of direction into our conduct in life. When these powers are drawn up into awareness, they are transformed into conscious knowledge, concepts and ideas—and then they bring blessing, become wholesome, give us direction and aim, tranquillity and certainty in life. This is a singular law and, it has to be acknowledged, one that is hard to comprehend. And yet it is true: while the insights of spiritual science can grant their possessor deep fulfilment when they enter his conscious mind, nevertheless they remain an element that renders us uncertain, that destabilizes us when they reside only below, unconscious, in dark regions of the soul. When what spiritual science seeks to raise into vivid awareness rests in these unconscious regions, it exerts no effect upon the human I; instead it surges in the sub-conscious and can have no influence on our experiences of happiness or pain, of success or disappointment. And then we can only bring to bear on these experiences of happiness or unhappiness the part of our being that is drawn into and along with them, and thus we lose ourselves in joy, succumb to pain, are intoxicated by success, filled with suffering by our disappointments. The soul is pulled hither and thither by all this, rocks and floats at random in the currents of life. But if the powers of spiritual perception that reside below in the dark regions of the soul are drawn up, if our I can bring these spiritual insights with it when life smiles upon us in good fortune, when life brings us pain and suffering, then the I no longer floats aimlessly upon the surge, is no longer pulled hither and thither by happiness or unhappiness. Instead it bears a strengthened inner life into fortune and misfortune, into pain and suffering, and gives us a different experience of them.

If we are to actually use what I have described, however, we will need to understand something about the nature of happiness and suffering, success and the lack of it. What in fact causes us happiness or unhappiness?

We cannot properly perceive what we experience when happy, when we enjoy success, in joyous moments, or when we feel pain or sadness, or suffer moments of disappoint-ment, unless we realize that two aspects constitute us—an external physical one and an inner, soul-spiritual element. What is happiness? What is the experience of success?

Depending on whether we are happy or in pain, the interplay of our supersensible aspects changes subtly. When we feel happy, and when our soul immerses itself in this experience, or likewise when it plunges into the delight of success, what otherwise rests and resides within us erupts from within and is borne away on the success or happiness that enter us. We become divorced from our inner being and cease to be entirely within ourselves. Instead we enter an alien element. Becoming detached from and out of ourselves in this way is, as it were, a swing of the inner pendulum in one direction. When we experience pain, by contrast, or disappointment then the soul and spirit, as if fleeing pain and failure, withdraw deeper inside us than they would normally do in our ordinary way of being. It is as if the soul and spirit tense and cramp, contract; and so, instead of losing ourselves to the outer world as we do in joy and gratification, we withdraw deeper within us. And since it is our nature to find peace and fulfilment only when we are in harmonious connection with the world, both this contracted inner state and its opposite, an evaporation into joy, unbalance this harmony and estrange us from our intrinsic being. In pain the inner pendulum swings in the opposite direction from joy: we flee from the world, and seek to live entirely within ourselves. Actually this swinging back and forth is part and parcel of all human experience, and necessary to it; it is just a matter of how we experience it. In fact, if we do not experience it we seek it. And in passing I want to show how we may actually *seek* the estrangement we experience quite naturally in happiness, which, as we see, is a condition in which we are no longer fully within ourselves but subsumed in an element estranged from our true I.

This will be the case when someone does not wish to acknowledge what is actually contained in this I, when he does not wish to let what it contains rise into his awareness but instead immerses himself in another element and numbs himself to the truth of the I by resting instead in the external world. And in our time we see—let me add this— the saddest examples of such a search, of such self-estrangement and effort to immerse oneself in a realm that does not belong to the I, a refusal to acknowledge the true form of the I. It can happen that whole masses of people are seized by such a feeling, by the desire to intoxicate themselves with something other than what is intrinsically conveyed by the I. Let's imagine the following scenario. A number of people who have had an inner sense for decades that they need redress for something that was taken from them—redress for themselves. Let us imagine that a moment comes when these people refuse to acknowledge what resides in their true I, that they seek to get beyond it, to find something that tips them over and intoxicates them; and now they no longer just seek redress, but say instead, 'Let us fight, join battle for freedom and our national rights!' This is nothing other than pushing the pendulum towards one extreme, that of intoxication. Or, another example. For decades people sing 'Rule Britannia' and the rest of that song, and at a certain point this suddenly swings to an extreme: they no longer stay centred, stable with the inmost form of the I, but find it necessary to depart from their intrinsic being and say, 'Let us wage war to secure our freedom and national rights!'

This has an addictive quality and can suddenly affect whole swathes of people like an epidemic: the quest to intoxicate themselves with what they seize hold of outwardly because they do not wish to stay within their I. Yet we only find our aim and direction, our assurance in life when we know how to stay within the I, and then also learn to bear it with us into all good fortune and all suffering, into all success and disappointment. The consolidation of this I, the securing and empowering of it inwardly, is something we achieve when we draw forth what renders this I unstable. It is rendered unstable by spirit perception that remains in dark regions of the soul and forms something like a heaving, rocking vessel as long as it stays down there, but gives us assurance in life when it is, as it were, raised up to a different place—into our conscious awareness. [...]

We cannot invariably feel this. But it is possible to try approaching things like this: that when we encounter happiness or good fortune which would otherwise intoxicate us, captivate and imprison us, we experience it fully, allow it full scope but then bear ourselves, with a strengthened inwardness of soul, with our empowered inner being, into this happiness. Or we experience a pain or grief fully, but learn to go down into it, to bear our I into it without estranging ourselves from the world. We carry our I with us into the pain.

To understand fully what this different approach to happiness or suffering means in life, it is necessary to look more deeply into the science of the spirit. The state arising in the soul that we can call 'clairvoyance'—as long as we do not misunderstand it—can be seen as an awakening through which we enter a world of which we knew nothing as long as we only had physical views of the world, rational judgements about it. Let us imagine that someone suddenly 'awoke' in this way when he was in the very midst of great joy or good fortune. Let us picture someone who previously was only used to thinking of the world in physical terms and physical effects upon him, immersing himself in it without the strength that spiritual science can give; let us imagine that he suddenly awoke in the midst of his success or good fortune, and saw the world of spirit. What exactly would he see?

Such awakening can become a deeply dark and disturbing moment in a life otherwise filled with happiness. At such a moment we perceive what I described: the soul's estrangement from itself. And the happiness or success that gave us such pleasure we see sinking away as it were, sinking so that we cannot hold on to it since we have no strength to do so. In particular such awakening can show us that we lose ourselves in life when, without spirit knowledge, we gallop ahead into happiness or success. You see, spiritual science shows us that what we attain in happiness and success can only become really empowering forces at work in our eternal I, which passes into eternity through the portal of death, when we do not lose ourselves but retain and preserve ourselves within the experience of happiness. Spiritual science does not seek to spoil or disparage the pleasure of human happiness. It does not want to diminish joy and happiness by one iota. But what it does seek to show is that a happiness experienced without the real connection to the world I characterized cannot unite its effects with the deepest powers of our I. Someone who goes through life and, without spirit knowledge, receives no strengthening of his I emerges from one happy occurrence with nothing more than a longing for another and yet another. He does not draw from one experience of happiness the strengthening powers it can give for all his subsequent life. If, instead, we bear into our happy experience the powers granted to us when we seek spirit knowledge, we suck from good fortune a sustaining and enlivening power that informs our I because we have strengthened it through spiritual science; and then we carry with us for all eternity what happiness and success can give us.

It is similar with pain, suffering and disappointment. Once again we can draw on spirit knowledge for an answer to the question as to what we would perceive if we suddenly awoke at the moment of the greatest suffering and pain, awoke, I mean, to what this means in the world of spirit. We would then see the effect of this hurt withdrawal from the world, this convulsive contraction. We would see a darkening of what is around us—spiritual darkening is what we would see if we suddenly awoke without having developed spirit knowledge; and this darkness would change again if our soul were strengthened by spiritual science so that we could bear it into the pain, engage with suffering through it. All grows bright for such a soul as it experiences this awakening. Passing through pain with spirit awareness, the soul gains victory over its suffering, over all disappointment. From such experience grows the fruit of pain and disappointment; and this fruit is an enhancement of knowledge and perception, is the permeation of knowledge with a consciousness of spiritual life.

This is why, in these lectures here, I have often described an experience that the spiritual researcher can have. Happiness and pleasure always—or at least usually—approach us from without. They appear as something that comes towards us. In great pain and suffering we withdraw into ourselves. Happiness is something we'd like to grasp, and pain something we want to flee. But we can only flee it by contracting inwardly. Now if you ask someone who has acquired some degree of spirit knowledge as an inner possession whether he would prefer to do without happiness and joy, or pain and suffering, he will tell you that he is deeply grateful to worlds of spirit for the happiness and joy he receives, but if he had to choose he would do without them. While he owes much to happiness and good fortune, he will say that the disappointments he has suffered have given him insight into the world. His knowledge, and what it has made him, are due to the pain he has suffered. He will tell you that he has found himself through pain, and that these difficult experiences have enabled him to form a harmonious relationship with the world.

This is how thoroughly we revise our views of pain and happiness once we gain a relationship to spirit knowledge. And an elixir of life, a living power of life flows into us when we receive divine, spiritual forces into our soul; and this elixir of life is tranquillity, equilibrium and assurance—such tranquillity, equilibrium and assurance that henceforth happiness and suffering, success and disappointment acquire a quite different meaning in our life.

What do they come to mean? Well, happiness, since it gives us our cohesion and sense of connection with the external world, means a strengthening of our whole being. Happiness flows into our sensibility and into our impulses of will. We do not dismiss or disparage happiness. We accept it gratefully from the hands of universal potencies, but we pass through it and onwards as if plucking eternal fruits from the tree of happiness—fruits for our will, fruits for our soul. When we are able to enjoy our happiness in this way, we learn that we do not therefore have any less an experience of it than someone who revels in it without spiritual awareness. But our experiences of happiness become subtler and more intimate because they form a window, as it were, into a world of spirit; because they mediate to us the strengthening of soul that we can receive from spiritual worlds.

[...] But just as our will and sensibility can be strengthened by happiness, so from pain flows a strengthening of our knowledge and insight, our certainty of perception; we gain strength and assurance in another part of our soul, more than can accrue from happiness. In the same way that a martyr, as he dies in pain, seizes the victory of light over darkness, so someone who bears his spirit-conscious I into pain perceives how this I raises itself above pain. But as it does so, this spirit-conscious I grows ever more luminous, filling itself with light to become a beacon standing firm amidst the storms and travails of life.

[...]

If we pursue such knowledge we can come to identify our life, our I, with destiny. We are our destiny, for it has made us what we are. This can become apparent to us even without spirit knowledge. But if we enlarge this insight with spiritual perception, with the knowledge gained from spiritual science, so that we bear our I into the happiness and suffering that destiny offers us, then we fully enter the circumstances that fate brings us. And whereas we have found that we need, as it were, to detach ourselves from happiness and pain so that they do not become all-consuming, we find the opposite when we consider our destiny, and all that fate faces us with. It had to approach us as it did, and it came about through ourselves! You see, everything accomplished by destiny is intimately connected with our I. Gradually we unite consciously with our destiny: we grow together with it; we bear our I into the course of our destiny. We detach ourselves from our immediate experience but enter into our destiny and in doing so pass outwards into the unfolding course of the world. We become one with the world's motion, and enter knowingly into the stream of life. We immerse ourselves selflessly in what we otherwise regard only with sympathy and antipathy. Whereas before we regarded happiness with sympathy and misfortune with antipathy, in future we will know that destiny is something which we are immersed in, and if we were not we would not have become what we now are!

What I have described is easier to say than to do. But when we bear our I into the course of destiny, the question of destiny will become something quite different from what it normally is in life. It comes alive, kindles powers within us. In the same way that spiritual knowledge makes space in our soul to allow divine, spiritual forces to flow into us, and this gives us a sense of invigoration, so now there flows into the I—previously emptied and made open for destined circumstances or events—what passes through birth and death, what leads us back to former lives on earth, and shows us this present life as the point of departure for future lives. By no other means can we unite with our eternal nature and being, which passes through births and deaths, than by becoming one with the flow and course of destiny, realizing that we have often previously prepared our destiny, that we did so for this life too in our previous lives. We unite with what connects us with spirit within our soul. And whereas we otherwise float, as it were, in a lone vessel upon an infinite ocean, knowing nothing except what is happening here within this boat or in its close vicinity, through spiritual knowledge we learn that there are many other vessels on the waves in one direction, and many more in the other. We realize that our life in this single vessel—travelling between birth and death— will continue for a certain period but then, lifted from the forces that bind us to the life in this vessel, we will pass through a life in the spiritual world, and after a period will live once again in a different vessel, just as we lived in a different one previously. In the same way that we might feel unsafe if we thought we were bound to one boat alone but gain a sense of security from knowing that we can step from this into another, so life becomes more assured and certain within the eternal stream of existence when we place ourselves into our destiny in this way by identifying with it, uniting our I with it. What we experience in life, what approaches us as our karma, our destiny, grows to be what we have become in life. We learn to see the question of destiny as the question of how to perfect our soul. And we recognize that when we experience pain, suffering, disappointment, these sufferings strengthen the part of our soul where our conscious forces live. With this strengthened soul we pass through the portal of death, and bear these strengthened powers with us as we enter upon a different life. Whereas the question of destiny otherwise veils our gaze in darkness, it becomes the question of perfecting our soul once we penetrate it with spirit knowledge. And then, if we can approach the question of destiny in this way, inner tranquillity fills our life. [. . .]

All References to Happiness in Rudolf Steiner's Works

'The greatest possible happiness for all'—a devilish phrase[6]

The question of what drives and motivates people easily becomes the question of what makes them happy, and this gives the issue of happiness a quite particular hue. This is why you will find at various places in the fifth post-Atlantean epoch, especially in western culture, that people start expending much effort on considering the problem of happiness, on how to make life happy. This is subject to the influences I described earlier. For instance, we see here how people enquire into what should be done to ensure the greatest possible happiness in their lives on earth. The creation of earthly happiness becomes an ideal. As I said, this is not solely due to ahrimanic influences, for the ordinary progressive powers are also at work here. Naturally people *should* think about happiness. But through Ahriman's influence these enquiries acquired a certain hue, embodied in a really devilish phrase: 'The greatest good is the happiness of the greatest number of people on earth.' It is diabolical because it defines good in terms of, and in relation only to, happiness—that of the largest possible number too, which would mean the misery of the minority. This is roughly like developing an organism only down to the knees, and letting it waste away from there on. But even more than this, the conflation of happiness and goodness, happiness and virtue, reveals the ahrimanic trait here. Happiness and virtue, happiness and human good: the best minds in ancient Greece would have been quite unable to conflate these two concepts. But the ahrimanic influence in the fifth post-Atlantean epoch created an outlook which seeks good as embodied in happiness. Everything that you are familiar with as Saint-Simonism, the various endeavours to establish national economies, especially in western Europe, must be seen in this light; and only then can you understand what is at work here. Even Rousseau-ism is not free of this impulse. One has to study such things with a sober eye.

The I could not live in a culture of happiness[7]

In the West, there is a danger of people becoming entangled in sense life, which would divest this life of the I. You see, if the sole endeavour is to establish happiness on earth, the I could not live on earth. If good is to be founded only by spreading happiness everywhere, the following would happen, as the case of ancient Atlantis shows. In the middle of the Atlantean era, too, there were great impulses afoot that would ultimately have led to a kind of happiness. The impetus to good as people initially experienced it, was, in its form and effects, at first felt to offer a certain happiness. People give themselves up to happiness and its pursuit, they become obsessed with it. And in relation to Atlantean culture, the earth had to be swept away in a sense, since people retained of good only the element of happiness. In the post-

Atlantean era, Ahriman now seeks to establish a culture of happiness. This would mean peeling the apple then throwing it away! Human 'I's could no longer live if there were only a culture of happiness. Happiness and good, happiness and virtue are not synonymous concepts.

Here we can gaze into deep secrets of life. Something legitimate—that is, establishing a culture whose outcome and consequences must of course lead to a certain degree of happiness—is turned on its head so that people think happiness itself is the primary, desirable goal.

The happiness of the individual is inseparable from the happiness of all [8]

Nowadays we can sum up how people live as follows. Even if people don't admit it they think it's possible for one individual to be happy despite others around him being unhappy. It is quite possible for someone to feel happy while others are unhappy. Even if people rationally concur with the idea that the highest dictates of morality require all to be happy, in practice people actually think that it is perfectly possible for a lone individual to be happy despite others suffering. At some point [...] humanity will reach a stage of moral evolution where it will be impossible for one person to feel happy as an individual when others are unhappy. 'The happiness of the individual is inseparable from the happiness of all.' This will eventually prevail... No person will be able to feel privately happy if his happiness is not part of the happiness of all.

The happiness of the individual is not possible without the happiness of the whole of society[9]

Many people today are not yet very exercised about enriching themselves at the cost of others, or living at others' expense. It is not just that people don't really include this fact in their moral self-evaluation, but they don't even think about it as an issue. If they did, they would find that people live far more at others' expense, and to others' detriment, than they can begin to imagine. In fact, we all live at others' expense. Gradually an awareness will develop that living at others' expense, in the immediate community too, is the same thing as some organ of the body developing—wrongly—at the cost of another organ, and that an individual's happiness is impossible without the happiness of the whole community. Naturally people are completely unaware of such a thing today, but gradually it should become a principle of human morality. Nowadays people seek their own personal fulfilment first and foremost, not realizing that they can really only thrive if all others enjoy happiness.

Joy and pain in spiritual awakening[10]

He who sustains himself within pain
perceives victorious knowledge.
He who sustains himself in joy
perceives a world that goes under
to create foundations.

If he who loses himself in joy
were suddenly to *awaken*
he would perceive how all
the life forces of happiness go under—
and he could not preserve what goes under.

Awakening in pain, we see what survives—
and can preserve what goes under.

Human beings do not strive for happiness, but to fulfil their task in life[11]

When the ethical philosophers of pessimism, citing evidence that there is more lack of pleasure in the world than pleasure, claim that we should therefore try to work selflessly for society and culture, they fail to see that human will is by nature left unaffected by this recognition. Human endeavour is governed by the degree to which we can overcome all obstacles to our possible fulfilment. Hope of such fulfilment is the reason for human activity. Each individual's work, and all cultural endeavour, springs from this hope. Ethical pessimism believes that it must teach humankind that the quest for happiness is an impossible one, so that we can instead devote ourselves to ethical and moral tasks. But these moral tasks are nothing other than tangible natural and spiritual promptings, whose fulfilment is sought despite the lack of pleasure this incurs. The quest for happiness, which pessimism seeks to eradicate, does not in fact exist at all. We accomplish the tasks we have to because we *want* to do so through the inner strength and energy at work in us if we really perceive our own nature. Ethical pessimism claims that a person can only dedicate himself to what he perceives to be his life's task once he has relinquished the quest for enjoyment. But no ethical imperative can dream up life tasks and ethical ideals other than those whose realization or fulfilment human desires demand. No ethical dictate can deprive someone of the enjoyment that he finds in fulfilling what he thus desires. When the pessimist says, 'Don't seek enjoyment, for you can never attain it; instead strive to fulfil what you perceive to be your task,' we can reply: 'It is human error, and the invention of a misguided philosophy to claim that people seek only happiness.' No, they seek fulfilment of what their being requires or desires, and they focus on the tangible objects of this endeavour, and not on some abstract 'happiness'. And fulfilling this aim is pleasurable. When ethical pessimism urges us not to seek enjoyment but to accomplish what we perceive as our task in life, it has in fact highlighted what a person really *desires and wills* in line with his true nature.

Finding happiness through geometry—1[12]

I was profoundly satisfied to discover that one can live inwardly in the elaboration of forms perceived purely in the soul and devoid of impressions from the outward senses. This brought me solace for the mood that had arisen in me in consequence of my unanswered questions. To be able to comprehend something purely in the mind brought me inner happiness. It is true to say that geometry brought me my first experience of happiness.

Finding happiness through geometry—2[13]

The straight line that returns to itself as if in a circle struck me like a revelation. I left the lecture where this had first dawned on me with the feeling that a heavy weight had fallen from me—a sense of liberation. Once again geometry had brought me a sense of joyfulness as it had first done when I was young.

Happiness created by the free self[14]

What would become of divine freedom if nature were to lead us, as it were, by the reins and brood over us, care for us, nurture us always like young children? No, she must instead *deny* us everything so that, when we feel happiness, this is created entirely by the free self. Let nature daily destroy what we create so that we can daily take new pleasure in our creativity! Let us *owe nothing* to nature, and *everything* to ourselves!

Happiness and love attend our inner activity[15]

Happiness, joy, pleasure and fulfilment—the foundations of a healthy life—always spring from the same source, the sense of an inner life which accompanies productivity and inner activity. A person is happy when he can be active and engaged, though 'activity' need not be understood in a crass or overly physical way.

Why does love make us happy? It is an activity in which we may often not perceive activity as such, because this activity proceeds from within outwards and encompasses the other. Here we let our inwardness stream out, and this is why love is healing and brings us happiness.

The highest freedom—the greatest happiness[16]

If we call this perception of the highest truths our harmony with the absolute, we find that our highest freedom blossoms in it. We find ourselves at a point in the universe, a standpoint, and now there comes what we were discussing back in the winter: from here we survey the world, judging it, judging ourselves; and we are content with ourselves, with the world and everything in it. In the highest freedom manifests the greatest happiness, the fullest contentment. The human being has recognized his destiny and is reconciled with everything.

Happiness not the aim—1[17]

I have been reflecting on many of your words last Monday, before you left. Dear Anna, please do not think that I seek what people call *happiness*. I am happy to relinquish happiness. To think that I seek it is a misunderstanding. I want to work and act, to do whatever I can. And nothing more than this. I'll write again soon. Most warmly, your Rudolf.

Happiness not the aim—2[18]

But dear Anna, recently you yourself have seen everything mistakenly. Otherwise you could not have said you wish I could be happy. Do not misunderstand me. I know how you mean it. But I really do not seek to be personally happy. I only wish to be understood. My own person is something people should leave to one side.

Happiness not the aim—3[19]

Dear Anna, you must not suffer. Try to understand that I have a task in life governed by no personal motives. All I can do is keep saying this: I wish for nothing, least of all what so many people call happiness. Such happiness is nothing to me. I wish only to work and act.

Happiness and unhappiness are not absolutes[20]

If we are to understand each other,
Accustom yourself to change the sense
Of certain words. And do not be surprised
If in my speech what you call pain
Must have a different name.
[...]
I find you fortunate.
    (Benedictus to Capesius in *The Soul's Probation*)

Creating happiness from within[21]

We must create happiness and fulfilment from within ourselves, rather than waiting for it to come towards us.

Happiness must be achieved by our own efforts[22]

But let us not forget that pain is the herald of happiness. Think of mothers: how the joy they feel when their children flourish is sweetened by the cares, sufferings and efforts they have made. Any more thoughtful person would inevitably reject a happiness offered him by some external power; and this is because he cannot feel an undeserved gift as happiness. If some Creator figure had set to work to fashion the human being with the idea of endowing his creation with happiness as a universal legacy, he would have done better to refrain from making man at all. Human dignity is enhanced by the fact that whatever we create is always cruelly destroyed. We must always create and form things anew; and in activity lies our happiness—in whatever we ourselves achieve and accomplish. A happiness given is like a truth simply revealed. Only our own efforts to find the truth are worthy of us. Neither past experience nor revelation should govern us. When people recognize this fully, then revelatory religions will become a thing of the past. Then people will no longer even want God to reveal himself to them or shower his blessings upon them. They will want to perceive things through their own thinking, to find happiness through their own efforts. Whether some higher power guides our destiny for good or ill does not concern us—we ourselves must decide on the route we are to follow. The loftiest idea of God remains one that assumes that after creating the human being God withdrew from the world and left his latest creations entirely to their own devices.

Notes

1. Lao Tzu: *Tao te King. Das Buch des Alten vom Sinn und Leben* [Tao te Ching]. Translated into German by Richard Wilhelm, Munich 1978, section 58.
2. GA 28, pp. 20f.
3. GA 14, p. 160.
4. GA 61, pp. 164–93.
5. GA 64, pp. 186–207.
6. Lecture in Dornach, 24 September 1916, GA 171, pp. 108f.
7. Lecture in Dornach, 24 September 1916, GA 171, pp. 112f.
8. Lecture in Nuremberg, 27 June 1908, GA 104, pp. 203f.
9. Lecture in Berlin, 19 March 1918. GA 181, p. 111.
10. Notebook, January 1915, GA 40, p. 129.
11. GA 4, pp. 230f., Chapter XIII: 'Der Wert des Lebens'.
12. GA 28, p. 21.
13. Ibid. p. 64.
14. Ibid. p. 131 (quoted from 'Nature and Our Ideals').
15. Lecture in Munich, 5 December 1907, GA 56, p. 221.
16. Letter to Rudolf Ronsperger, 16 August 1881, GA 38, pp. 30f.
17. Letter to Anna Steiner-Eunike, 6 February 1904, GA 39, p. 433.
18. Letter to Anna Steiner-Eunike, 14 February 1904, ibid. p. 434.
19. Letter to Anna Steiner-Eunike, 11 April 1904, ibid. p. 436.
20. GA 14, p. 160.
21. 'Die geistige Signatur der Gegenwart', GA 31, p. 256.
22. GA 1, pp. 124f.

Sources

The following volumes are cited in this book. Where relevant, published editions of equivalent English translations are indicated. The works of Rudolf Steiner are listed with the volume numbers of the complete works in German, the *Gesamtausgabe* (GA), as published by Rudolf Steiner Verlag, Dornach, Switzerland.

RSP = Rudolf Steiner Press, UK
AP / SB = Anthroposophic Press / SteinerBooks, USA

GA

1   *Nature's Open Secret* (SB)
4   *The Philosophy of Freedom* (RSP)
14   *Four Mystery Dramas* (SB)
28   *Autobiography* (SB)
31   *Gesammelte Aufsätze zur Kultur- und Zeitgeschichte 1887–1901* ('Essays on Culture and History 1887–1901')
38   *Briefe Band I: 1881–1890* ('Letters, volume I: 1881–1890')
39   *Briefe Band II: 1890–1925* ('Letters, volume II: 1890–1925')
40   *Truth-Wrought Words* (RSP)
56   *Die Erkenntnis der Seele und des Geistes* ('Knowledge of the Soul and the Spirit')
61   *Menschengeschichte im Lichte der Geistesforschung* ('Human History in the Light of Spiritual Research')
64   *Aus schicksaltragender Zeit* ('At a Time of Grievous Destiny')
104   *The Apocalypse of St John* (RSP)
171   *Innere Entwicklungsimpulse der Menschheit. Goethe und die Krisis des neunzehnten Jahrhunderts* ('Inner Evolutionary Impulses in Humanity')
181   *Dying Earth and Living Cosmos* (RSP)

All English-language titles are available via Rudolf Steiner Press, UK (www.rudolfsteinerpress.com) or SteinerBooks, USA (www.steinerbooks.org)

Steiner

A NOTE FROM RUDOLF STEINER PRESS

We are an independent publisher and registered charity (non-profit organisation) dedicated to making available the work of Rudolf Steiner in English translation. We care a great deal about the content of our books and have hundreds of titles available – as printed books, ebooks and in audio formats.

As a publisher devoted to anthroposophy...

🗝 We continually commission translations of previously unpublished works by Rudolf Steiner and invest in re-translating, editing and improving our editions.

🗝 We are committed to making anthroposophy available to all by publishing introductory books as well as contemporary research.

🗝 Our new print editions and ebooks are carefully checked and proofread for accuracy, and converted into all formats for all platforms.

🗝 Our translations are officially authorised by Rudolf Steiner's estate in Dornach, Switzerland, to whom we pay royalties on sales, thus assisting their critical work.

So, look out for Rudolf Steiner Press as a mark of quality and support us today by buying our books, or contact us should you wish to sponsor specific titles or to support the charity with a gift or legacy.

office@rudolfsteinerpress.com
Join our e-mailing list at www.rudolfsteinerpress.com

🗝 RUDOLF STEINER PRESS